EDITOR: LEE JOHN

MW00603951

OSPREY MILITARY

MEN-AT-ARMS

THE BRITISH TROOPS IN THE INDIAN MUTINY 1857-59

Text by
MICHAEL BARTHORP
Colour plates by
DOUGLAS N ANDERSON

First published in Great Britain in 1994
by Osprey, an imprint of Reed Consumer Books Limited
Michelin House, 81 Fulham Road,
London SW3 6RB
and Auckland, Melbourne, Singapore and Toronto

ISBN 1 85532 369 9

Filmset in Great Britain by Keyspools Ltd, Golborne,
Lancashire
Printed through Bookbuilders Ltd, Hong Kong

Artist's note

Readers may care to note that the original paintings
from which the colour plates in this book were
prepared are available for private sale. All
reproduction copyright whatsoever is retained by the
publisher. Enquiries should be addressed to:

Douglas N. Anderson
37 Hyndland Road
Glasgow
G12 9UY

The publishers regret that they can enter into no
correspondence upon this matter.

Author's note

Readers may find it helpful to consult this title in
parallel with the following Osprey publications:

MAA 196 *The British Army on Campaign (2):
1854–56*
MAA 198 *The British Army on Campaign (3):
1856–61*
MAA 219 *Queen Victoria's Enemies (3): India*

THE INDIAN MUTINY

INTRODUCTION

In 1856 the British Army emerged from its first conflict with a major power since 1815 – the Crimean War. Though victory over the Russians had been won, the war revealed many defects in the British military system which ideally would require a period of peace to repair. Disputes with Persia and China were brewing; but should these come to force of arms, the force needed would not be large, nor should it unduly delay or interrupt the reforming process. Yet within 14 months of the Peace of Paris being signed with Russia, the Army was faced with a crisis which, before it was finally resolved, would require an even greater commitment of force than the Crimean War had. From May 1857 British rule in northern India became seriously threatened by mutiny or unreliability in the largest military force maintained in the sub-continent – an insurrection which sundry princes and notables saw as their opportunity to regain lost power and property.

British India, which still embraced a diminishing number of semi-independent or 'protected' states, was nominally ruled through its Governor-General – from 1856, Lord Canning – by the East India Company (EIC), whose Court of Directors in London was answerable to the British Government's Board of Control, whose President was a political appointment and had a seat in the Cabinet.

The rule of the previous Governor-General, Lord Dalhousie, had not only advanced the boundaries of British India to the Afghan border by its final conquest of the Sikhs of the Punjab and that territory's annexation in 1849; but had been marked by Dalhousie's determination to bring peace, prosperity and justice to ordinary Indians, together with the benefits of modern communications, irrigation, education and trade. Though Dalhousie's reforms were undoubtedly well-intentioned, their execution was at times hurried and heavy-handed; and, unlike some who knew India better, he did not appreciate what dangers might lie in what Sir George MacMunn has called trying 'to graft Western progress on an Eastern stalk'. Such a process bore hardest on local rulers and landowners, whose methods were remote from Dalhousie's liberal ideals but were at least familiar to their subjects and tenants. When, in pursuit of eradicating misrule, he annexed the deeply corrupt Kingdom of Oudh, a large and predomi-

Troops advancing towards Delhi.

3

nantly Hindu province ruled by a Moslem dynasty, in 1856, his action not only exacerbated the fears and distrust of other rulers, but caused resentment within parts of the EIC armies, much of which were recruited from the sons of high-caste Hindu land-owners and agricultural yeomen of Oudh, and on which British power ultimately depended.

The three separate EIC armies of Bengal, Madras and Bombay, part-European but mostly Native, have been described in MAA 219, *Queen Victoria's Enemies (3)*. With 135 major units[1] the Bengal Army was larger than the other two combined (120 major units). Separate from the Bengal Army was the Punjab Irregular Force (16 units). In addition there were the Oudh Irregulars (17 units), formed from the King of Oudh's disbanded soldiery; and 'Contingents' of all arms, with British officers, belonging to the protected states, of which the two largest were those of Gwalior and Hyderabad. Finally there were a number of cavalry regiments and infantry battalions of the Royal, or Queen's Army, stationed in India 'on loan' to the EIC. These should have totalled 26; but five had been sent to the Crimea and only one replaced, and by 1857 three had gone to Persia. On the eve of the Mutiny the grand total of Native troops stood at 311,000, of Europeans (EIC and Queen's) 40,000 – a proportion of eight to one.

The Bengal Army was not only the largest but also the most susceptible to disaffection. What brought it to insurrection, thereby giving other disaffected elements the opportunity to rebel, has been explained in MAA 219. For reasons of space this will not be repeated here; but it is important to emphasise that the famous matter of the greased cartridges[2] was but the spark that ignited an already explosive situation which nevertheless caught most of the British authorities unawares.

A factor which later greatly affected the balance of forces must be mentioned. The sudden, perilous predicament facing the EIC might well have seemed the opportunity for the recently conquered but still martial Sikhs to regain their independence.

---

1 Cavalry regiments, artillery horse brigades or foot battalions, infantry battalions.

2 See post, under Weapons.

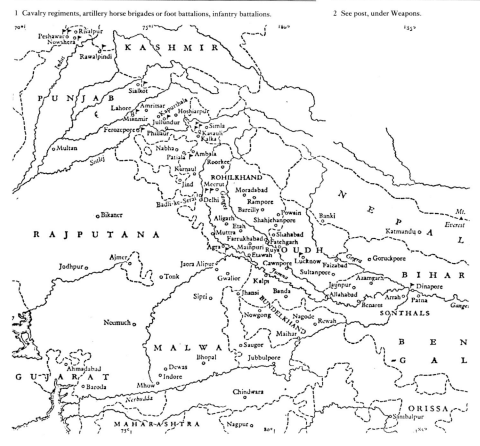

The theatre of operations, 1857–59. The black flags indicate locations of Queen's troops in the Bengal Presidency in May 1857.

However, the Bengal sepoys had not, on the whole, performed well in the Sikh Wars, the hardest work of two very hard campaigns falling to the Queen's regiments; and during these operations considerable mutual respect had developed between British and Sikhs. The Punjab's subsequent occupation by Bengal regiments was unpopular with both sepoys and Sikhs: the former because as high-caste Hindus they regarded the Sikhs as unclean barbarians, the latter because they considered themselves the better soldiers. Both felt contempt for each other, but the sepoys also felt fear – and the Sikhs knew it. British administration of the Punjab since 1849 had been sound and fair. To many Sikhs, 1857 seemed the chance not to turn against their new masters, but to win the return match against the Bengal sepoys.

OUTLINE OF OPERATIONS

The operations to suppress the Mutiny fell into three major campaigns. After the regiments at Meerut mutinied, they marched to **Delhi**, only 40 miles away. This had a large garrison of Bengal Native Infantry (BNI) with no British regiments and, above all, was the seat of the old King of Delhi, Bahadur Shah, descendant of the great Mughal emperors. The Meerut men, quickly joined by the Delhi regiments, proclaimed him Emperor of India, providing a focus of rebellion at the ancient Mughal capital, to which mutineers and dissidents from all over the region were drawn.

The retention of Delhi, as a symbol of success, became as vital to the rebel cause as its recapture was to the British. The latter's concentration of sufficient force was hampered by logistic unpreparedness and the need to ensure the security of the Punjab and the Afghan frontier. Eventually it was recaptured, against heavy odds; and this proved the turning point of the rebellion, leading to the relief of Agra, the EIC's headquarters in the North-West Provinces.

The concurrent campaign in **Oudh** involved the efforts to relieve the small garrison besieged in Lucknow, the province's former capital and seat of the British Resident, and, unsuccessfully, the smaller garrison at Cawnpore, the head of the vital commun-

Bugler Hawthorne, HM 52nd Light Infantry, winning the VC at the storming of the Kashmir Gate, Delhi: painting by Vereker Hamilton. (Anne S.K. Brown Military Collection)

ications up the Ganges from Calcutta, through which any relief force for Lucknow had to pass. The massacre of the Cawnpore garrison, with their wives and children, through the treachery of one of the revolt's major leaders, the Nana Sahib, inspired the advancing British troops to merciless revenge and superhuman efforts to overcome great hardship and dangers. Again the problems of concentrating sufficient force, in this case from outside India, and the need to suppress outbreaks en route, delayed the relief of Lucknow, Havelock's first attempt only managing to reinforce the garrison, Campbell's second terminating with its evacuation. The latter was followed by the battles at Cawnpore against the mutinied Gwalior Contingent, which had joined the Nana's general, Tantia Tope. With Cawnpore

Queen's infantry in hand-to-hand fighting at the Jumma Masjid mosque, Delhi.

secured, Campbell prepared for Lucknow's final capture in March 1858. He failed to prevent thousands of rebels escaping into Oudh and its neighbouring areas of Rohilkand and Bihar, which took the rest of the year to pacify.

The third campaign, of **Central India**, occurred south of the Delhi-Oudh operations, in the Malwa area of protected native states, including Gwalior, and the recently annexed Jhansi, lying between Rajputana and Bundelkhund. Mutinies and uprisings began in June 1857, but owing to a dearth of European troops and a particularly heavy monsoon Sir Hugh Rose could not start major operations until January 1858. These, which included the Bombay Army and Hyderabad Contingent as well as British forces, were directed first to the capture of Jhansi, whose Rani was joined by Tantia Tope, then to the pursuit of the rebel forces who, after their defeat at Kalpi, occupied Gwalior town and fort. Here they were finally defeated in June 1858. Until the end of

the year, and into 1859, operations continued to suppress guerrilla activity and, in particular, to capture Tantia Tope, who was finally taken in April 1859.

CHRONOLOGY

1857

Jan.	Rumours of greased Enfield cartridges, affecting Hindus and Moslems, at Dum Dum.
Feb.–May	Mutinies or disbandment of four Bengal regiments.
May 10–11	Mutinies and murders at Meerut and Delhi.
12–29	Mutinies at 12 stations in Ganges Valley. BNI regiments in Punjab disarmed by Brig. Gen. Nicholson's moveable column (into July).
17	Delhi Field Force (FF) advances from Ambala.
30	Outbreak at Lucknow; mutineers dispersed or disarmed.
31	Mutinies in Rohilkand.
June	Further mutinies throughout month in Ganges Valley, Rajputana, Central India (CI).
5	Mutiny at Cawnpore. Maj. Gen. Wheeler's entrenchment besieged.
8	Delhi FF, plus Meerut garrison, defeat mutineers at Badli-ke-Serai, reach Delhi Ridge; siege begins 15 June. Massacre at Jhansi (CI). Malwa FF begins operations in CI.
11	Col. Neill's force from Calcutta for relief of Cawnpore reaches Allahabad.
25	Nana Sahib offers Wheeler terms at Cawnpore. Garrison massacred, women and children imprisoned.
30	Sir H. Lawrence, commanding at Lucknow, defeated at Chinhut by advancing mutineers. Lucknow Residency besieged.
July	Mutinies in Punjab, Malwa, Ganges Valley, Agra. Siege of Delhi and Defence of Lucknow continue.

7	Maj. Gen. Havelock and Neill leave Allahabad for Cawnpore.	*Sept. 2*	Maj. Gen. Outram reaches Allahabad with reinforcements.
15	British women and children in Cawnpore murdered.	*4*	Siege Train reaches Delhi.
16	Havelock defeats Nana Sahib, First Battle of Cawnpore.	*14–20*	Assault and capture of Delhi.
		15	Outram joins Havelock.
25	Havelock resumes advance, defeating rebels at Unao (29 July).	*19*	Havelock and Outram advance on Lucknow.
Aug.	Further mutinies in CI, Bihar. Siege of Delhi and Defence of Lucknow continue.	*25*	First Relief of Lucknow. Enlarged garrison remains besieged, with outlying detachment at Alambagh.
2	Malwa FF relieves Mhow.	*Oct.*	Defence of Lucknow continues. Campbell prepares relief. Unrest in North Bengal and Bihar.
5–13	Havelock forced by casualties to return to Cawnpore.		
14	Nicholson and moveable column arrive Delhi Ridge.	*10*	Part of Delhi FF relieves Agra, marches to join Campbell.
16	Havelock defeats enemy at Bithur but unable to advance. All Oudh now in rebellion.	*15*	Revolt in Kotah (Rajputana).
17	Gen. Sir Colin Campbell arrives India as C-in-C.		

Bombardier Thomas, Bengal Artillery, winning the VC for rescuing a wounded Madras Fusilier during a sortie by that regiment, HM 78th and dismounted Probyn's Horse from the Lucknow Residency, 27 Sept. 1857. (Modern painting by Dawn Waring for 55 (Residency) Battery, RA)

Nov. 9–12	Campbell advances from Cawnpore to Alambagh.	Rose clears country east of Saugor; advances on Jhansi.
9–19	Tantia Tope with Gwalior Contingent advances on Cawnpore, held by Maj. Gen. Windham.	*Mar. 1–10* Campbell reaches Alambagh. Preliminary operations against Lucknow.
14–17	Second Relief of Lucknow.	*11–21* Assault and capture of Lucknow. Rebels escape to west.
19–27	Evacuation of Lucknow, leaving garrison at Alambagh. Campbell marches for Cawnpore.	*21–31* Rose reaches Jhansi, begins siege.
24	Malwa FF completes operations south of River Narbada.	*29* Rajputana FF takes Kotah.
26–28	Second Battle of Cawnpore. Windham attacks Tantia Tope but forced to retreat.	*April* Campbell begins pacification of Oudh; expeditions into Bihar to relieve Azimgarh and into Rohilkand.
28–30	Campbell reaches Cawnpore to join Windham.	*1* Battle of the Betwa. Rose defeats Tantia Tope marching to Jhansi's aid.
Dec. 6	Third Battle of Cawnpore. Campbell defeats Tantia Tope.	*3–5* Capture of Jhansi.
7–31	Operations to capture Fatehgarh, NW of Cawnpore.	*25* Rose advances towards Kalpi.
16	Maj. Gen. Sir Hugh Rose takes command of CI FF.	*May* Rose continues advance. Rohilkand operations continue.

1858

Jan. 6	Fatehgarh captured. Campbell prepares capture of Lucknow.	*5* Battle of Bareilly. Campbell defeats rebels but they escape.
16	Rose begins CI campaign with relief of Saugor (3 Feb.). Rajputana FF operates to west.	*7* Rose defeats Tantia Tope at Kunch.
		19–23 Rose attacks and captures Kalpi.
Feb.	Campbell concentrates on N bank of Ganges for entry into Oudh.	*22* Rohilkand operations completed. Guerrilla warfare begins.
		June Anti-guerrilla operations in Oudh, Bihar and on Nepal frontier.
		1 Tantia Tope and Rani of Jhansi seize Gwalior.
		5 Rose leaves Kalpi for Gwalior.
		16 Rose attacks rebels at Morar.

Left: Meeting of Havelock, Outram and Campbell, second relief of Lucknow, 17 Nov. 1857: after the painting by T.J. Barker. (National Army Museum)

Above: Windham's attack on the Gwalior Contingent, second Battle of Cawnpore, 26 Nov. 1857: lithograph after Captain D.S. Greene, R.A. (Anne S.K. Brown Military Collection)

17	Battle of Kotah-ke-Serai. Rajputana FF defeat rebels. Rani of Jhansi killed.
18–20	Rose captures Gwalior. Tantia Tope flees.
July–Dec.	Mopping-up operations and hunt for Tantia Tope in Rajputana and CI.

1859

Jan.–Mar.	Pursuit of Tantia Tope continues.
April 7	Tantia Tope captured; executed 18 April.

THE OPPOSING ARMIES

Rebel Forces

These have been covered at some length in MAA 219, but can be summarised as follows:

(a) The Bengal Army, of whose 123 Native Regular, Irregular and Local units, 59 mutinied and 37 partially mutinied, or were disarmed or disbanded. In the Regular category, of 88 cavalry, artillery and infantry units, 50 mutinied and 33 partially mutinied.

(b) The Oudh Irregular Force (14 units).

(c) 'Contingents' of some protected states.

(d) Retainers of Oudh's and other notables.

(e) Bands of Moslem fanatics, including Arab and Afghan mercenaries.

(f) Criminal elements.

MAA 219 gives no total under arms, which is impossible to assess, but some approximations of rebel strengths at certain events can be given:

(a) Delhi when assaulted held some 40,000 with 150 guns.

(b) Lucknow before its final capture held 120,000 (excluding civilians).

(c) At Bareilly, May 1858, 36,000, 40 guns.

(d) In Jhansi, April 1858, 11,000 with Tantia Tope's 20,000 approaching.

A comparison of these strengths with those of the EIC forces opposing them on each occasion reveals a rebel superiority, on average, of 6.25:1. A major reason why such superiority so often failed to win victory was the rebel weakness in leadership at battalion level and above, and the lack of any proper command structure to co-ordinate their operations.

East India Company (EIC) Forces

With the Bengal Army mutinous, or at best unpredictable, and with the intentions, at least early on, of the Bombay and Madras Armies uncertain, the only forces that could be relied upon for immediate action were the Company Europeans and the Queen's regiments then in India.

Company Europeans

In Bengal these totalled only three brigades of horse artillery (54 guns); six battalions of foot artillery finding 11 field batteries (66 guns) and 13 garrison companies; and three battalions of infantry. Bombay and Madras had the same infantry, but only one brigade of horse artillery each, and three and four battalions respectively of foot artillery. All three had European engineer officers and NCOs.

Queen's Regiments

In 1857 the British cavalry and infantry totalled 23 regiments and 107 battalions, exclusive of the Household Cavalry and Foot Guards. Between 1858 and 1859 two new regiments and 25 battalions were raised[1]. When the Mutiny began four regiments and 18 battalions were based in India but, of these, HM 14th Light Dragoons, HM 64th Foot and 78th Highlanders were serving in Persia. Furthermore, the 19 units in garrison were not evenly distributed. Between Calcutta and Cawnpore (over 600 miles by road) there were only HM 53rd Foot at Calcutta and HM 10th Foot at Dinapore. HM 32nd were at Lucknow, and HM 6th Dragoon Guards and 60th Rifles at Meerut. Except for four units in the Madras and Bombay Presidencies, all the rest, plus most of the Bengal Europeans, were in the Punjab, between Ambala (130 miles from Meerut) and Peshawar (400 miles to the north-west).

This concentration of the most reliable troops, under the most effective British officers and officials then in India, certainly ensured the border and prevented any repetition of Meerut and Lucknow in the Punjab, as well as having salutary effects on the province's inhabitants; but it delayed action being taken further south, where the outbreaks created a barrier between the Punjab and Bengal proper.

Nevertheless, it was from the Punjab and Meerut that the force which eventually captured Delhi came. Delhi's fall released some of this force for operations in Oudh, but it was still deemed necessary to keep a proportion of Queen's regiments in the Punjab and on the Frontier where some, like HM 70th, remained throughout the Mutiny. Therefore, to find sufficient strength to subdue the rebellion further south and in Central India, other Queen's units had to be brought

in: those from Persia, from Burma (3), Ceylon (1), the diverted China expedition ($4\frac{1}{2}$), and ultimately from more distant garrisons and England – all of which took time.

Much of the Army in England had not long since returned from the Crimea and was regaining its strength, both numerically and figuratively. But so serious did the position in India appear that reinforcements had to go, even if many were little more than recruits. Between 1857 and 1859, eight cavalry regiments, 47 infantry battalions, the newly formed Military Train[2] and, for the first time since the 18th century, four troops RHA, 26 companies RA, and four companies RE, were despatched from Australia, the Cape, Mediterranean and England. By the end of the Mutiny 64% of the entire 1857 strength of Queen's Cavalry and Infantry (excluding Household troops) were serving in India, although at least a third were only engaged on the periphery of the main operations or were occupying garrisons vacated by units in the field;[3] nevertheless this was 16% more than had been employed in the Crimea.

Notwithstanding this considerable force, the time it took to assemble, plus the size of the operational theatre, meant that the task could not

---

1 5th Lancers, 18th Hussars, 2nd Battalions for the 2nd–25th Foot, 100th Foot.

2 Formerly Land Transport Corps, employed as cavalry in India.
3 For regiments engaged, see MAA 198, p5.

Left: Officers and men of EIC Bengal Horse Artillery before the Mutiny: lithograph after H. Martens. (Private collection)

Right: EIC 1st European Bengal Fusiliers repulsing mutineers at Delhi: lithograph after Captain G.F. Atkinson.

have been accomplished without other forces – those that remained loyal to the EIC or were prepared to enlist in its cause.

Loyal Native Forces

The Bombay Army, except for two regiments, remained loyal and, as mentioned earlier, played a major role, with the Hyderabad Contingent, in Central India. No mutinies occurred in the Madras Army, which had a subsidiary role in Central India and sent a few troops to the Oudh campaign. Of the Bengal Army, three Irregular cavalry regiments, four of BNI, plus elements of three others, remained loyal, as did the three Gurkha battalions, most of three Sikh units, seven other Local or Irregular infantry units, and two Native artillery sub-units.

The most important accession to EIC strength, both as regards the security of the north-west and major operations, came from the Punjab Irregular Force: the Corps of Guides, five cavalry regiments and ten infantry battalions. Raised in 1846–49, it was recruited entirely from what later became known as 'the martial races' – Sikhs, Punjabi Mussulmen, Gurkhas, Pathans, Afghans and Baluchis, who felt no kinship or respect for the Hindu sepoys.

In addition, others of their ilk, particularly Sikhs for reasons already stated, came forward to form new Irregular cavalry units, like Hodson's and Probyn's

Horse, and 14 battalions of Punjab infantry. Although their loyalty was often given more to individual British officers than to the company, they provided valuable reinforcements, the cavalry particularly off-setting the EIC forces' shortage of that arm. Such units also provided employment for British officers of mutinied or disbanded regiments.

Tactics

The Crimean lessons of the rifle's greatly improved range and accuracy over the smoothbore musket had not yet begun to influence the Army's tactical methods and formations, which remained essentially those in force in the Crimea, despite a new 'Infantry Manual' issued in 1857. These, and the handling of cavalry and artillery, have been explained in outline in MAA 196 (pp. 9–18), and their application to the Mutiny fighting in MAA 198 (pp. 7–8), and space does not permit their repetition here. Though not all of the EIC forces yet had the rifle, its advantages over the sepoys' smoothbores soon became sufficiently evident to most commanders. This, added to the open nature of much of the terrain, resulted in a greater use of skirmishing lines rather than close-order formations. In the cavalry too, particularly the newly raised Irregulars, much looser formations became the norm, partly due to their men's nature and partly to their hasty training, many learning their trade almost as they went along.

However, old habits died hard. In one instance the sight of HM 53rd, armed with Enfields, advancing in column of companies against infantry and artillery at Lucknow, caused a wrathful explosion from Sir Colin Campbell to a staff officer: 'Go down and tell that commanding officer to deploy at once and advance in skirmishing order. How can men be such fools!'

Since the rebels' sepoy regiments had been trained in the same methods, the earlier fighting became a conflict between those methods, at least while the sepoys retained their regimental organisation. But, more often than not, the EIC forces' better and more experienced command structure, their superior rifle-fire, and not least the dogged determination of the British soldier, prevailed against the massed ranks of sepoys and their allies, notwithstanding their usually well-served artillery. When it is remembered that tactical thinking conventionally demands an attacker to have a 3:1 superiority over a defender to ensure success, the fact that the Delhi Field Force took the city with an inferiority of 1:9 illustrates the strengths and weaknesses of both sides. Furthermore, not only were the EIC forces usually outnumbered, they were also having to contend with a suffocating climate, for which they were not inured nor well-equipped.

DRESS, EQUIPMENT AND WEAPONS

This subject, as it affects the rebel forces, has been covered in MAA 219, so will not be considered further here. Some examples are, however, shown in Plate A to provide a contrast with the Queen's and loyal EIC troops that occupy the other plates.

The nature of campaigning in the Mutiny, and particularly the fact that much of it occurred in the hottest time of the year, resulted in a variety of costumes being adopted, many of which, especially among Queen's troops, bore little resemblance to the dress required by regulations. In the Sikh Wars a decade earlier the troops had largely fought in regulation dress. The Mutiny was very different, although even then some regiments had no alternative to their home service dress, as will be seen. To understand what was actually worn in the field, the regulation clothing must first be explained.

Queen's Troops
In 1857 the Army's dress had not long entered the 'tunic era'. The 1855 dress changes had abolished, for all arms except the Royal Horse Artillery, the by then

old-fashioned coatees and jackets which ended at the waist in front but with long or short tails behind (see MAA 196). In their place had come the full-skirted tunic, double-breasted for lancers and infantry, single-breasted for the remainder, though the infantry changed to the latter from 1856. The tunic colour remained as before: scarlet (red for rank and file) for General and Staff Officers, Heavy Cavalry, Royal Engineers, and infantry, except for the 60th Rifles and Rifle Brigade in rifle-green; blue for other cavalry, Royal Artillery, and the newly formed Services (Military Train, Medical, Ordnance). Infantry bandsmen's tunics were white, but drummers and Light Infantry buglers wore red and Highland pipers green. Highland regiments, kilted and non-kilted, received the doublet with Inverness skirts, also at first double-breasted. Rifles officers' tunics followed the Light Dragoon pattern. Trousers remained as before, except the infantry's summer pattern changed to dark blue, white being retained for hot climates.

Except in the Heavy Cavalry, headdress changed to generally smaller and lighter patterns, the Light Dragoons and infantry retaining shakos but tilted forward in the French style, the infantry's still having front and rear peaks. In the three non-kilted Highland regiments, the 71st's and 74th's shakos followed the French trend, but the 72nd kept to the feather bonnet of other Highlanders. The lower busbies and caps for hussars and lancers were not authorised until 1857 and 1856 respectively. The Royal Artillery and Royal Engineers both adopted busbies in place of shakos, but the Military Train had shakos similar to Light Dragoons.

Examples of these uniforms for cavalry, artillery and infantry can be seen in the accompanying G.H. Thomas prints (for Engineers and Military Train, see MAA 198, p.21). Of particular note is the unique dress of the 6th Dragoon Guards, a Mutiny regiment, which wore a Heavy Cavalry helmet and a Light Dragoon tunic.

Undress uniforms underwent less alteration from the 1855 changes, although the infantry's Kilmarnock caps reduced slightly in height and their officers' caps received flat peaks. Highland regiments' undress headgear was now officially the Glengarry though some, like the 42nd, 71st, 72nd and 78th – all in the Mutiny – retained their old Kilmarnocks, known as 'hummle bonnets'. Mounted arms' 'pill-box' caps remained unchanged. The undress upper garment continued to be the shell or stable jacket, in the tunic colour with regimental facings, terminating at the waist with no tails. In Highland regiments officers and senior NCOs had scarlet shells, but those of sergeants and below were white. Officers on parade with troops wore shell or stable jackets, but for other undress occasions dark blue frock coats, also much used by General and Staff officers.

Left: A Queen's infantry battalion at full strength: HM 35th in column of companies in Indian cold-weather dress. The Band, Drums and Pioneers are at left. (Charles Stadden Collection)

Right: Officers and men of HM Rifle Brigade in forage caps and tunics. The 2nd and 3rd Battalions reached India in time for the Cawnpore battles in November and December 1857. (Rifle Brigade Museum Trust)

This dress and undress clothing pertained wherever British troops were stationed, both home and abroad, for peace and war. There could, however, be lengthy delays between the authorisation of new items and their actual issue, due in part to distance from the home base, in part to the requirement for using up and wearing out of old kit, each garment having a prescribed length of life between issues. For example, the order changing the infantry's tunics from double- to single-breasted was dated 28 March 1856 but was not to take effect until 1 April 1857. A tunic was renewed every year at home, but only every two years in India, as it was worn less there. Thus a soldier in India who received a new double-breasted tunic on 1 April 1856 (after the change had been published) would not receive his new, single-breasted garment until 1 April 1858, two years after authorisation.

Another 1856 order, of 1 September, stated that in future regiments in India would receive, instead of a shell jacket, a red serge or kersey frock, cut like a loose tunic but with fewer buttons and embellishments. However, as shells also had a two-year life, the earliest an infantryman could have received a new frock would have been 1 April 1858, by which time he would be in hot-weather clothing. Thus, despite frocks being authorised well before the Mutiny began, it is unlikely that they were worn during it – except possibly by officers who, being responsible for the provision of their own uniforms, were sometimes in possession of new patterns before their men.

In India the home service clothing sufficed during the so-called 'cold weather', (October to March) when temperatures were roughly equivalent to a good English summer. (It was, incidentally, the season to which most of the Sikh Wars had been confined.) For the hot weather, when temperatures soared into the 90s and 100s (Fahrenheit), troops were issued with white cap covers and a number of white drill shell jackets and trousers. Another item peculiar to India were trousers of Nanking cotton or dungaree material, which were issued to soldiers primarily as a working dress but which had been used for field service in the campaigns of the 1840s.

In those days Queen's regiments customarily spent a dozen years or more in India (the 9th Lancers for example, were there from 1841 until 1859), so their men became acclimatised; but even so few parades occurred during the heat of the day in the hot weather in peacetime. Yet it was during that very season that much of the hardest fighting and marching in the Mutiny took place. Before seeing how the regulation cold- and hot-weather dress was adapted to cope with such conditions, the dress of loyal EIC troops, and the accoutrements and weapons of both elements, must next be considered.

Loyal EIC Troops

In principle the dress of the EIC Armies followed the Royal Army's, both for dress and undress, cold and hot weather, except where there was no equivalent, as in the Irregular corps and the Punjab Irregular Force

Left: Hodson's Horse in action against mounted rebels at Rhotuck, near Delhi: lithograph after Captain G.F. Atkinson. (National Army Museum)

Right: The Military Train acting as cavalry engaging sepoys at Lucknow: painting by C.C.P. Lawson. (Ann S.K. Brown Military Collection)

(PIF). Dress changes, however, tended to be promulgated later. For example, the 'Albert' shako, worn by Queen's Infantry and the Royal Artillery until 1855, was approved at home on 4 December 1843, but not until 29 June 1846 for EIC European Infantry and Foot Artillery, who still had it as their dress headgear in 1857. Shakos had been abolished in favour of Kilmarnock forage caps for Indian ranks in the Bengal and Bombay Native Infantry in 1847 and 1854 respectively, Madras NI continuing to wear their bulbous-shaped black turbans. The major change, to the tunic, was not approved by the EIC until three days before the Mutiny broke out at Meerut, and then only for infantry and artillery. Thus, in 1857, the Regular EIC regiments, European and Native, still had, when parading in dress, a pre-1855 appearance compared with Queen's troops.

One unique item, uninfluenced by Royal Army fashions, was the headdress worn by Europeans of the three Presidencies' Horse Artilleries who, instead of the RHA's busby, had a glazed 'Roman' helmet with brass crest and horsehair mane, the colour of which, and the embellishments, varied between the three regiments.

The dress of the PIF cavalry and infantry followed a completely different line from the European-style dress of the Regular regiments and adopted a more indigenous costume, with 'lungis' or 'pagris' (turbans) round their heads, smock-like

'alkalaks' or 'kurtas', and the loose trousers called 'pyjamas', although there is evidence of shell jackets and simple frocks being worn. Among the PIF cavalry, and the new regiments raised in the Punjab during the Mutiny, there were many variations of cut and colour. The PIF infantry generally followed the precedent set by the Corps of Guides, the first regiment in India, Queen's or EIC, to adopt loose clothing of khaki colour, or drab as it was officially called. The only exception was the 1st Punjab Infantry, who wore loose drill frocks and trousers dyed a dark indigo. The keynote of all such uniforms was practicality.

The three Gurkha battalions existing in 1857, though not then officially designated as 'Rifles', had worn dark green uniforms for some years, the cut of which, by the Mutiny, approximated to that worn pre-1855 by HM Rifle Brigade, though with Kilmarnock forage caps (see Osprey Elite 49, *The Gurkhas*).

The Madras and Bombay Light Cavalry's European-style uniforms were, like those of Bengal, 'French grey'. The Bombay Irregular cavalry, like the Scinde Horse, followed the trend of the PIF cavalry. Among the Bombay Infantry in its forage caps and red coatees, the Baluch Battalion struck an unusual note with green turbans, green, red-laced frocks, and red trousers.

Since Indian troops were born to the climate and since, at least in the PIF and Irregular corps, their clothing was better suited to it, their dress required less adaptation and departure from regulations than that of the Queen's regiments.

Accoutrements

Personal accoutrements for all arms remained as they had been at the end of the Crimean War (MAA 196), although some minor modifications were authorised in 1856–57. The materials were buff leather, normally pipeclayed, for all belts and slings, and black leather for pouches, except for Rifles who had all in black.

The cavalryman received a waistbelt with slings for his sword and, for hussars only, his sabretache, and a shoulder belt with pouch for his carbine or (officers and all lancers) pistol ammunition. Carbine-armed cavalrymen had an extension to the pouch belt suspending a clip for attachment to the carbine's side-bar. Following the adoption of the tunic, the waistbelt was worn under it by the 6th Dragoon Guards, Light Dragoons and hussars. Officers' dress belts were gold-laced but in undress plain white; their pouches, more ornate than the men's, varied according to their branch and were the same in dress and undress.

The infantryman had his waistbelt to suspend his bayonet from a straight-hanging frog at the left hip, and a 40-round pouch suspended from a shoulder belt, the pouch hanging about four fingers' width below the right elbow. The waistbelt was put on over the shoulder belt. The main pouch was supplemented by a 20-round expense pouch carried on the waistbelt to the right of the clasp; in this position it afforded easier access to the soldier and was topped up from the main pouch. Some regiments may still have had the old 60-round pouch, for which no

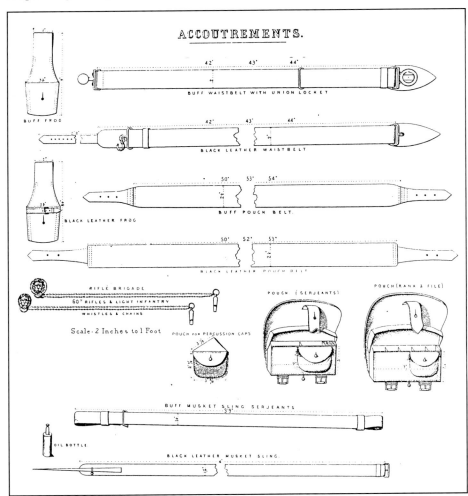

Infantry frogs, waistbelts, pouch belts, pouches and slings.

expense pouch was issued. Attached to the front of the pouch belt was a buff leather cap pouch, although regiments with the old equipment had brown leather cap pouches attached to the waistbelt. Cap pouches were also issued to carbine-armed cavalry.

A new pattern knapsack had been approved in 1854, but in India these were always transported for the men. An infantryman's belts and pouches, when full, together with his rifle and bayonet, gave him a weight of 21 lbs to carry, exclusive of his rations and whatever else he may have fitted into his haversack. This container, made of coarse linen, had formerly only been issued when required as an item of 'camp equipage', but from 1856 had been a regular issue to each man; it was carried slung over the right shoulder outside the waistbelt. The soldier's issue water bottle was still the antiquated wooden container of the Napoleonic War, but these seem not to have been provided in India, where water carriage and supply was the duty of the regimental 'bhisties' with their water-skins. However, during the Mutiny individual water containers were acquired by some regiments, made of local soda-water bottles covered in leather

and suspended from a leather strap over the left shoulder.

Since the tunic's introduction the only accoutrements required by regulations for infantry officers were the waistbelt, of enamelled white leather, with slings for the sword, which served for both dress and undress, thereby dispensing with the old shoulder belt, as worn by company officers in dress, and the black leather undress waistbelt. Rifles' officers wore their black sword belts under the tunic and additionally had a pouch belt bearing their regimental crest. Highland officers retained their shoulder belts with slings for the broadsword and had a waistbelt for the dirk. When on service an officer might add a revolver holster, field glasses, a haversack and whatever else he might think necessary, but such additions were a matter for him and his purse.

Accoutrements of gunners and sappers were essentially those of either cavalry or infantry, with minor differences, depending on whether the wearer was normally mounted, as in the RHA or RA drivers, or dismounted.

The accoutrements of EIC Regular units fol-

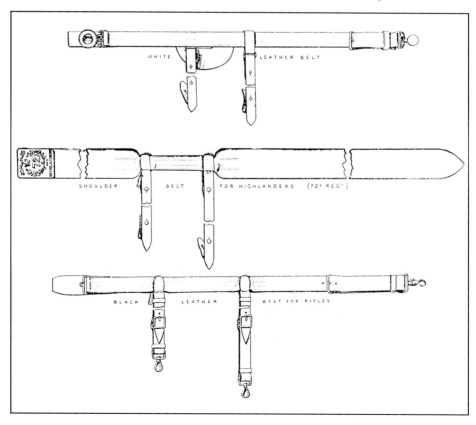

Infantry officers' sword belts. From top: Line waistbelt, Highlanders' shoulder belt, Rifles' waistbelt.

lowed those of Queen's regiments but, as with uniform, were taken into use later. For example, the Bengal Fusiliers in 1857 still had the old pouches and their officers the black undress waistbelts. A variety of sword and pouch belts was used by the Irregular cavalry, particularly those raised in 1857, who initially had to make do with whatever was available. In the PIF infantry, and comparable troops like the Baluch Battalion, brown leather was more commonly used for belts and pouches, though black was provided for Gurkhas.

Weapons

In the Crimean War the Minié rifle had proved a battle-winning weapon in the British infantry's hands until it was superseded, in the later stages of the war, by the 1853 pattern Enfield rifle (see MAA 198, p.23). The Enfield, single-shot and muzzle-loading, had a 39-in. barrel, or 33-in. for the short version issued to sergeants and Rifles; weighed 8 lbs 14½ ozs (the short, 8 lbs 4½ ozs); was of .577-in. calibre, and was sighted to 1,200 yards. The long version had a 17-in. socket bayonet, the short a 22¾-in. sword bayonet. Its average rate of fire was two rounds per minute.

The British battalions sent to India as reinforcements were equipped with the Enfield. For those already in India the situation varied, some having it, others not, or having a limited number. HM 75th Regiment, for example, received 100 Enfields in mid-May 1857 while on the march to Delhi, but were not fully equipped with it until February 1858, when its share of operations was over. Since the Minié rifle was never issued in India, most Queen's battalions who had been there for some years still had the 1842 smoothbore, percussion musket. With the same barrel and bayonet length as the Enfield, it was of .753-in. calibre, weighed 10 lbs 3 ozs, but was only accurate up to 200 yards – less than a quarter of the Enfield's range (see MAA 193, p.24).

This musket was also the EIC infantry's arm, although other weapons were used by the PIF and Gurkhas (see commentaries to Plates B3, C2). It had been intended to re-arm the EIC battalions with the Enfield in 1857 and partial issues had been made. However, its three-grooved barrel necessitated the greasing of its cartridges to assist loading. Since the loading drill required the end of the cartridge to be

bitten off, and since the grease was believed by both Hindus and Moslems to be compounded of animal fats of deep significance to both religions, this proved to be the spark which converted the underlying fears and resentments of the Bengal sowars and sepoys into open mutiny. In rejecting the Enfield, they embarked upon insurrection with an inferior weapon.

Several cavalry carbines had been under trial since 1855 to find a replacement for the smoothbore, muzzle-loading, 1842 percussion Victoria, as used in the Crimean War and still in general use. This had a 26-in. barrel, was of .733-in. calibre, and weighed 7 lbs 9 ozs. The only two carbine-armed Queen's regiments in India, the 6th Dragoon Guards and 14th Light Dragoons, had this weapon, the 9th and 12th Lancers having the 1842 Lancer pistol. One of the carbines on trial, the American breech-loading Sharps, was issued to the 2nd Dragoon Guards, the 7th and 8th Hussars before leaving for India in 1857. It had an 18-in. barrel and was of .577-in. calibre.

The outbreak at Meerut began with the refusal by sowars of the 3rd Bengal Light Cavalry to handle cartridges at a parade to learn the new loading drill. This might suggest that they, and other EIC cavalry, were being armed with some new, rifled carbine. In fact their carbines were smoothbore and the cartridges of the old pattern, but the sowars' fears were too deep-seated for them to take the cartridges—

though this did not prevent them using the same ammunition after they had mutinied. There was no carbine version of the Enfield in India at that time.

There was much variety among the firearms of Irregular cavalry, particularly those raised in 1857, owing to the 'silladar' system under which they were recruited and equipped (see MAA 219, p.22). The matchlock was a fairly common type; and the Scinde Horse uniquely had double-barrelled carbines. The same applied to their swords, which were usually of the indigenous type known as 'tulwars'. Often these were supplemented by lances.

Swords of Queen's Cavalry and Royal Horse Artillery were officially of the universal 1853 pattern with three-bar guard. Their officers retained their 1821 Heavy or Light Cavalry patterns. The 1853 type may not have reached all regiments stationed in India, who would have had the earlier Light Cavalry pattern, as did the EIC Regular regiments.

Officers of Infantry, Royal and EIC Foot Artillery had the 1822 Infantry officers' sword with 'Gothic' hilt in brass, steel for Rifles. Highland officers of course had broadswords.

The regulation lance was the 9-ft. ash pole with steel point and shoe, fitted with a buff leather arm sling and red-and-white pennon. Some lancer officers equipped themselves with hog-spears.

Turning from personal weapons to the artillery's crew-served armament, the weapons remained the same muzzle-loading smoothbores, with the same ammunition, as used in the Crimean War (see MAA 196, pp.15–18). The calibres of all guns, howitzers and mortars were standardised between the Royal and EIC artilleries, but there were differences of design. Whereas the EIC 9-pdr. gun and 24-pdr. howitzer were shorter and lighter than the RA equivalents, the EIC carriages were heavier and more cumbersome. They also had two axle-tree seats, which would not be a feature of RA guns for another decade and a half.

Both Royal and EIC horse troops had 6-pdr. guns and 12-pdr. howitzers, the field batteries 9-pdr. guns and 24-pdr. howitzers, but the proportion of guns to howitzers per troop/battery varied – 4:2 (Royal) and 5:1 (EIC). Of position guns, the siege train sent to Delhi included eight 18-pdrs., six 24-

Right: Infantry officers' swords, scabbards and knots. From top: Highlanders, Line, Rifles.

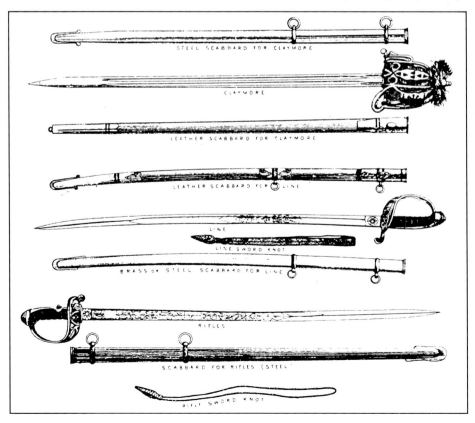

Left: Captain Brownlow, with British officer and sepoy of his new regiment of Punjabis raised in 1857: artist unknown. (Anne S.K. Brown Military Collection)

Left: Infantry and cavalry of the Punjab Irregular Force with a mountain battery: watercolour, 'The Artillery Train' by W. Carpenter. (Private Scottish collection)

Right: HM Cavalry, full dress. From left (M = in Mutiny): 6th Dragoons, 6th Dragoon Guards (M), 2nd Dragoons, 11th Hussars, 17th Lancers (M), 8th Hussars (M). (After G.H. Thomas)

pdrs., six 8-in. howitzers, and of mortars, four 10-in., four 8-in., and six $5\frac{1}{2}$-in. The position guns for Campbell's relief and capture of Lucknow were supplemented by the Naval Brigade from HMS *Shannon* manning six 64-pdrs., two 24-pdr. howitzers, and two 9-pdrs., plus two rocket launchers.

All Royal guns/howitzers, and their accompanying wagons, were drawn by three or more pairs of horses, each pair having its own driver on the nearside. The same applied in EIC horse troops, but in some EIC field batteries and position gun detachments bullocks were used in lieu. In Royal, Madras and Bombay horse troops the gunners were individually mounted, but in the Bengal HA they rode the offside draught horses.

DRESS ON SERVICE

The plates and commentaries thereto illustrate and describe the dress worn by various ranks of certain regiments in the operations at Delhi (Plates B and C), in Oudh (D, E and F), and in Central India (G and H). To supplement these, some general remarks and notes on other regiments' dress follow.

Since the Mutiny broke out in May, well into the hot season, the first troops to be engaged – those that came to form the **Delhi** Field Force – were, with some exceptions, in their white drill clothing. Some commanding officers realised how impractical this would be for hard campaigning before even reaching Delhi. HM 52nd Light Infantry dyed their whites khaki before leaving Sialkot on 25 May to join the Punjab Moveable Column, and HM 75th (Plate C3) did likewise at Ambala on the same date. Their example, and the appearance of PIF regiments like the Guides and 4th Punjab Infantry (B3), inspired most of the force to follow suit. The Hindustani word 'khak' meant 'dust' and, as used by the PIF, was described as 'a sort of grey drab, being nearly the colour of the desert or the bare stony hills'. But the rudimentary dyeing methods used resulted in 'so many different shades – puce colour, slate, drab – not only in the different corps, but in men belonging to the same company'. HM 61st's once-white shell jackets were described by Lieutenant Sloman as 'blueish-brown', being worn with trousers of the same hue or the blue dungaree type.

In some regiments the men's shirts were dyed as well and the jackets discarded (see C1). HM 52nd wore their shirts outside their trousers in the Indian fashion. In modern times 'shirt-sleeve order' is a common form of military dress, but in those days the sight of British soldiers in shirt-sleeves, except when off-duty, was so unusual as to be commented upon often by eye-witnesses. Indeed the whole appearance

of the Delhi troops was so extraordinary that later on, when HM 8th and 75th marched through Agra where, though confined in its fort, the European population had been little affected by the Mutiny, an Englishwoman exclaimed, 'Those dreadful-looking men must be Afghans!'

The most common form of headdress was the Kilmarnock forage cap, with cover and curtain (C1). In some regiments, like HM 61st, the men's caps had peaks like the officers'; in others, like HM 52nd and 75th (C3), it was common practice to add a rolled turban or 'pagri' to the cap. Sun helmets had first made the odd appearance in the Sikh Wars, but at this stage of the Mutiny they were still fairly rare, being confined to commanders, staff and officers of EIC regiments (see B1 and MAA 198, Plate A2). One of Captain Atkinson's Delhi lithographs shows gunners and drivers of the Bengal HA apparently wearing them, but a contemporary drawing of the Bengal HA at Bareilly in 1858 has them in covered forage caps. Since Atkinson's original drawings were lithographed by another hand, it may be that the sun helmets were a misinterpretation of the gunners' Roman helmets with white covers, with which the

lithographer was unfamiliar. Orders for large numbers of sun helmets to equip all ranks were not placed with native contractors until 1858.

Captain Griffiths, HM 61st, deplored how, at Delhi, 'many corps had become quite regardless of appearance, entirely discarding all pretensions to uniformity and adopting the most nondescript dress'. However, there were exceptions. HM 9th Lancers abjured the use of khaki dyes and, throughout the Mutiny, proved an exception to Griffiths' criticism (see commentaries to E2). The 1st Punjab Infantry and Sirmoor Goorkhas (C2) kept their dark uniforms, although the Kumaon Gurkhas adopted khaki. Owing to a shortage of transport for baggage, the troops from Meerut – HM 6th Dragoon Guards (Carabiniers), 60th Rifles (B2) and Tombs' troop of Bengal Horse Artillery – marched to Delhi in cold-weather clothing. Captain Anson, 9th Lancers, described 'the poor Carabiniers' as looking 'dreadfully heavy and oppressed' in their blue clothing, though whether they were in tunics or stable jackets is unclear. The story of Tombs ordering his men to hack off the red collars of their dress jackets after leaving Meerut is often quoted. Despite the heat,

Royal Horse Artillery and
Royal Artillery, full dress.
(After G.H. Thomas)

HM 60th's surgeon believed that the riflemen's relative immunity from cholera, which so afflicted other regiments at Delhi, was due to their green jackets whose serge gave better protection from the sun's rays than the linen and drill worn by others.

As for officers on the Staff, Captain Medley, Bengal Engineers, summed up their appearance: 'no two men were dressed alike, all kinds of boots, trousers, and breeches of every description, coats of every variety of colour and cut, headdress including the turban, the helmet, the solar-topee, the wide-awake[1] and half a dozen others'. Seldom before in the British Army's history can there have been an assemblage of troops of such a variegated, rough-and-ready appearance as the Delhi Field Force. Perhaps the most notable aspect – considering that the Crimea, and the Sikh Wars before it, had been

fought in regulation dress or undress uniform – was that, as Medley noted, 'British scarlet [was] a rare sight indeed'.

This was not the case in the **Oudh** campaign from June 1857 to May 1858, the operations in and around Cawnpore and Lucknow, and later in Rohilkand and Bihar. One reason for this was that some five months of it coincided with the cold season; another was that, latterly, many regiments recently arrived from England were involved; and a third that some regiments, though based in the East, had for one reason or another no alternative to 'British scarlet'.

When Lucknow and Cawnpore first became besieged in mid-1857, HM 32nd was the only Queen's battalion in garrison at the former, with one company at the latter, and was, like the Delhi regiments, in its white drill (D1). The first relief force that could be assembled, under Havelock, included: HM 64th and 78th Highlanders, brought back from the Persian War; the first arrivals of the diverted China expedition, HM 5th Fusiliers and part of the

---

1 A broad-brimmed hat.

90th Light Infantry (seven companies); from Burma, HM 84th; and EIC Madras European Fusiliers, brought up to Calcutta from Madras. Plate D includes representatives of the Madras Fusiliers (D3) in the special clothing acquired before marching up from Calcutta; and of HM 90th (D2) in the 'boat-coat' supplied to UK-based elements of the China force – frocks of brown holland material with red facings, devised for the work expected on the Chinese rivers.

The regiments from Persia had returned with only their cold-weather uniforms. On leaving Allahabad on 3 July the 64th were ordered to march in shirt-sleeves, consigning the tunics worn hitherto to their kitbags. Five days later its Light Company was issued with some 'light clothing', though of what nature is uncertain. After reaching Cawnpore most of the battalion remained there in garrison, only two companies going on to Lucknow, attached to HM 84th. The orders issued by Havelock on 15 September for this advance required a tunic or shell jacket, with cloth trousers, to be packed in the men's bedding, implying they marched in shirt-sleeves with white or dungaree trousers. The 64th men remaining at Cawnpore were to receive 'two white tunics[sic]

each as soon as possible', perhaps the same as issued earlier to its Light Company. An advanced company of the 84th, which had been sent on in May to Lucknow before it was invested, had had to march in cloth uniforms without even forage cap covers, despite having reached Calcutta from Burma in March.

Before going to Persia the 78th Highlanders had left their feather bonnets at Poona and, since their return voyage took them straight to Calcutta, they went through the first relief of Lucknow in covered forage caps, red doublets still of the double-breasted cut, kilts and hose (see MAA 198, Plate A1). After the second relief and evacuation, the 78th became part of the Alambagh garrison; by February 1858 their Highland dress had become so worn out that they presented 'the most motley appearance'. Lieutenant Sankey, Madras Engineers, sketched one of them in a makeshift hat, apparently made of two net curtains over a cane frame, a loose white smock, and dungaree trousers.

HM Infantry, full dress. From left (M = in Mutiny): 41st (Bandsman), 10th (Drummer) (M), 55th, Rifle Brigade (M), 29th (Pioneer) (M), 32nd (Sergeant) (M), 78th (Piper and Corporal) (M). (After G.H. Thomas)

HM 5th Fusiliers had been stationed in Mauritius when ordered to China, so had not received the boat-coats issued at home. They went to Lucknow wearing ship's smocks issued for the voyage, of the type in Plate F2, over white trousers. Spare smocks were cut up to make covers and curtains for their forage caps, to which were added peaks removed from their shakos (see MAA 198, Plate A3). Two companies, which did not accompany Havelock's column, were in the second relief wearing red tunics and white trousers. After the final capture of Lucknow the 5th were issued with khaki cotton frocks and trousers, and by May 1858 were fully equipped with airpipe helmets.

The China boat-coats were also in evidence during the second relief, worn by HM 82nd and 93rd Highlanders. The 93rd wore them over their kilts, with hose and spats below, together with feather bonnets to which a quilted white cotton sunshade was attached. As only the NCOs and men were issued with these coats the 93rd's officers had to have theirs made up of alpaca material which, as one wrote, was 'by no means so serviceable'. One officer wore his shell jacket underneath, and another his doublet, to give extra warmth during the cold weather of 1857–58. The 93rd wore this kit through the final capture of Lucknow and during the subsequent operations in Rohilkand. At Lucknow all ranks carried their greatcoats rolled over one shoulder –

right for the men, and left for the officers; this, incidentally, saved several lives by serving as a kind of breastplate. All had the leather-covered water bottles.

HM 23rd Fusiliers, also of the China force and in Campbell's relief column, presumably had boat-coats although no record has come to light, and at the final capture in March they were observed in red.

Campbell's second relief column also included, from the Calcutta garrison, HM 53rd (Plate E1) and, from the Delhi Field Force, HM 8th and 75th (C3), EIC 2nd and 4th Punjab Infantry (B3) plus, among the mounted troops who were mainly Punjab Cavalry, HM 9th Lancers who had now gone into their cold-weather clothing (E2). The column's artillery, both Royal and EIC, was supplemented by the Naval Brigade from HMS *Shannon* (Plate E3).

Also in the force was the balance of HM 90th which, having been shipwrecked on the voyage out and lost all their kit, had been issued, on reaching India, with white jackets and trousers to supplement the varied clothing provided through public subscription among the Europeans of Singapore, where they had first landed with little more than a shirt to their backs.

By the time of the second and third battles of Cawnpore, more reinforcements from England had come up and were to form the bulk of the troops that fought these battles and the subsequent capture of

EIC 1st Punjab Infantry, Native officers and sepoys. (After Captain W. Fane)

Mutineers:
1: Sowar, 2nd Bengal Lt. Cavalry
2: Subadar, 12th Bengal Native Inf.
3: Sepoy, 54th Bengal Native Inf.

A

Delhi:
1: Officer, Bengal Artillery
2: Cpl., HM 1st Bn., 60th KRRC
3: Sepoy, 4th Punjab Infantry

B

Delhi:
1: Pte., 2nd Bengal Fusiliers
2: Sepoy, Sirmoor Bn.
3: Officer, HM 75th Rgt.

C

Lucknow, Sept. 1857:
1: Pte., HM 32nd Rgt.
2: Sgt., HM 90th Lt.Inf.
3: Officer, Madras Fusiliers

D

Lucknow/Cawnpore, Nov. 1857-March 1858:
1: Pte., HM 53rd Rgt.
2: Pte., HM 9th Lancers
3: Officer, Royal Navy

E

Oudh & Rohilkand, March-Aug. 1858:
1: Driver, RHA
2: Cpl., HM 79th Highlanders
3: Rissaldar, Hodson's Horse

F

Central India, Jan.-June 1858:
1: Pte., HM 14th Lt. Dragoons
2: Officer, HM 86th Rgt.
3: Gunner, Bombay Horse Artillery

1   2   3

Central India, March-Sept. 1858:
1: Pte., HM 72nd Highlanders
2: Pte., HM Rifle Bde. (Camel Corps)
3: Pte., HM 95th Rgt.

Lucknow, at which they were assisted by Outram's division of the battalions engaged in the earlier operations. An officer of the latter, the future Field-Marshal Garnet Wolseley, then a captain in the 90th, noticed how the recently arrived British regiments' 'smart clothing contrasted forcibly with the many-coloured "rags" in Outram's division of veterans'. Further contrast with the home service uniforms was provided by the Sikh and Punjabi regiments of horse and foot as, for example, Plates F3 and B3 respectively.

Unlikely though it may seem, considering that they were not acclimatised and that the March daytime temperature at Lucknow of over 90° Fahrenheit was higher than normal, the 2nd Dragoon Guards (Queen's Bays) were observed by several eye-witnesses to be wearing their scarlet tunics and brass

helmets, 'as if', one wrote, 'for the express purpose of catching the rays of the sun'.

Supporting the cavalry at Lucknow were two troops of Royal Horse Artillery in home service dress but without busbies, which had been left at Calcutta (Plate F1). In contrast, and exemplifying Wolseley's above-quoted observation, was the Bengal artillery-man, Captain Olpherts, whom he saw clad 'in a fez cap and a Turkish "grego" (coarse hooded jacket) tied round his waist with a length of rope, followed by his Battery-Sergeant-Major in a sort of shooting coat made from the green baize of a billiard table'.

In uniforms as thick as the Bays' and RHA's, but of a more sombre hue, were the 2nd and 3rd Battalions of HM Rifle Brigade, which had marched up to Cawnpore in their 'European cloth dress and shakos'. In accounts of the Cawnpore battles and

Captain Dighton Probyn, EIC 2nd Punjab Cavalry, winning the VC at Agra, 10 Oct. 1857: painting by W. Desanges.

Lucknow's capture are many references to the 'dark green of the Rifles', though it is unclear if they wore tunics or shell jackets and if shakos gave way to forage caps. After the fall of Lucknow the Rifles adopted hot-weather clothing of 'slate-coloured cotton' with regimental black facings (Plate H2).

An officer of HM 97th stated that his regiment, like the Rifles, marched up in tunics and covered shakos (see MAA 198, Plate B1), but exchanged the latter' for covered forage caps once operations at Lucknow began. Instead of tunics as worn by their men the 97th's officers had a scarlet frock, fastening with four buttons, with collar and pointed cuffs in the pale blue regimental facing colour. With this garment they wore their sashes over the left shoulder and the sword belt under the frock. A photograph of these officers, taken after the hot weather had set in, shows them in loose white frocks and trousers, with turbans wrapped round their forage caps.

A sergeant of HM 88th recalled fighting at Cawnpore in his red tunic. The correspondent W.H. Russell observed HM 38th covering a river crossing at Lucknow in 'red coats and white cap covers'. It seems likely that other new arrivals like HM 20th and 34th were dressed similarly. It is remarkable how these regiments from England functioned in the Lucknow fighting because, as Russell said, 'the heat was sweltering. I pitied our men as they stood under

its rays, many of them unprovided with proper protection against the sun, and retaining their old European outfit'.

Two more Highland regiments had now joined the 93rd: HM 42nd and 79th. Both retained their feather bonnets and at Lucknow were in red with kilts, hose and spats. W. Desanges' painting of Lieutenant Farquharson winning the VC on 9 March shows the 42nd in doublets, but the records of the 79th mention 'loose red serge jackets with green facings'. For the subsequent Rohilkand campaign the 79th adopted ship's smocks (Plate F2).

After the fall of Delhi and subsequent operations in its vicinity, EIC 1st European Bengal Fusiliers joined Campbell's army. Having been unable to obtain red tunics for the cold weather, the regiment was furnished with a supply of blue cloth from which tunics, or more likely frocks, were made up regimentally. These were worn at the capture of Lucknow. Afterwards, for the hot weather, officers received loose, slate-coloured frocks made of jean, piped blue round the collar and cuffs, with trousers of the same material. A photograph showing this costume also includes NCOs and men of the regiment wearing smocks and dark trousers.

After Lucknow's capture, the follow-up operations into Oudh, Rohilkand and Bihar coincided with the onset of the hot weather, with a consequent relinquishing of regulation clothing, as has already been noted above for some regiments. Lieutenant-Colonel H.H. Crealock, on Campbell's staff in

EIC Bombay Light Cavalry with the Rajputana Field Force: *watercolour by Lieutenant J.N. Crealock, HM 95th. (National Army Museum)*

EIC Bombay Horse Artillery and Bombay Native Infantry with the Rajputana Field Force: watercolour by Lieutenant J.N. Crealock, HM 95th. (National Army Museum)

Rohilkand, sketched HM 7th Hussars with turbans round their forage caps, loose, 'dust-coloured' frocks, and home service trousers. Another Crealock drawing, of the Bengal Horse Artillery at Bareilly, has been mentioned earlier in respect of their covered forage caps, which were worn with dyed white stable jackets and overalls (for an officer, see MAA 198, Plate B2). Most of the Staff officers drawn by Crealock, including Campbell himself, have airpipe helmets with substantial pagris, loose frocks probably drab and fastened by loops and olivets, and trousers either strapped down over Wellington boots or tucked into long Napoleon boots.

Included in the Azimgarh Field Force were HM 10th Foot, formerly of the Dinapore garrison and present at Lucknow in March, and HM 13th Light Infantry, which had arrived in India from the Cape the previous October. The 10th's surgeon, Gordon, recorded that the regiment marched in khaki trousers and woollen shirts with sleeves rolled up. A portrait of a 10th officer, William Fenwick, shows him in a helmet with a pagri around it, a four-button drab frock with open, step collar and matching trousers, his sword belt worn over the frock. Lord Mark Kerr, commanding the 13th, who had the eccentric habit of carrying his headdress in his hand, was observed thus by W.H. Russell in February and wearing a red, quilted calico jacket, 'his old Crimean blue stuff

trousers and long, untanned leather boots' – a somewhat bizarre appearance which caused a soldier of another regiment to incur his wrath for failing to recognise him as an officer. The same boots appear in a portrait of him at Azimgarh, but worn with a pale buff frock fastened with loops and olivets, and dark grey trousers; in his hand he carries his shako within a light grey cover and curtain, its green light infantry falling plume emerging through the top of the cover. His men wear the same headdress, pale grey frocks and dungaree trousers (see MAA 198, p.11).

Despite the April sun being, as Russell said, 'so fierce that it threatened to strike down any European in daytime', and with temperatures in tents at 100° Fahrenheit, some regiments were without light clothing. Ensign Parsons of HM 35th recalled marching in April from Dinapore against rebels in Bihar, the men in red tunics, the officers in shell jackets or kersey frocks, blue serge trousers, and forage caps with white cotton covers and surrounded 'save in front, with a stiff, starched white screen not unlike a lampshade'. Owing to the heat the march began at 3 a.m., but even so it was 'hot and stuffy'. Russell recalled 'the indescribable fatigue and monotony' of such night marches with nothing at the end but the sun 'which burns you like fire'.

Crealock sketched the Carabiniers in Rohilkand, still as they had been at Delhi, in their light dragoon

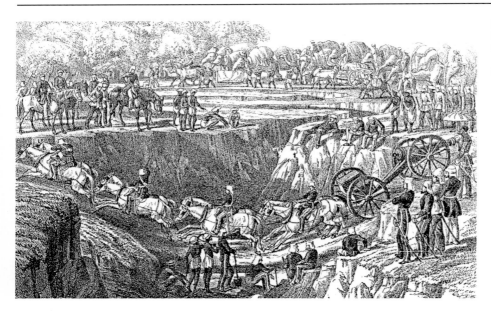

tunics, their only concession to the sun being covered forage caps instead of their brass helmets (see MAA 198, Plate B3). According to an Orlando Norie watercolour they fought in their cloth uniforms at Bareilly, a day which a 93rd officer described as 'the hottest upon which British soldiers were ever called upon to fight a general action'.

The Queen's troops engaged in the **Central India** campaign were, with the exception of HM 12th Lancers, 14th Light Dragoons (Plate G1) and 86th Foot (G2), reinforcements from England. One participant recorded that 1858 was the hottest year in India since 1812, yet some of these regiments had to march – over great distances – and fight in their cloth uniforms until May, and some later still.

HM 8th Hussars, though reaching India in December 1857, were not fully operational until February due to lack of horses. Besides the issue of Sharps carbines mentioned earlier, the regiment had received white cotton covers with peaks for their forage caps, but no other hot-weather clothing. With this headdress they had to wear their home service stable jackets and trousers, and were sketched so dressed by Lieutenant J.N. Crealock of HM 95th when with the Rajputana Field Force in June, when it had become really hot (see MAA 198, p.4). Another sketch, by Lieutenant Forteath of EIC Bombay Army, shows them still in the same kit in mid-August when pursuing Tantia Tope.

HM 17th Lancers did not take the field until the autumn of 1858 to join the same hunt. An officer of the 8th commented on the 17th's smartness when they came up, and a watercolour shows them in caps like the 8th's, home service tunics and trousers.

The shortage of cavalry for wide-ranging operations led to the use of units of camel-mounted infantry. One had been formed at Lucknow in April from men of HM 88th – who had now exchanged their red tunics for suits described by Surgeon Sylvester of the 14th Light Dragoons as 'of lavender hue' – and of the Rifle Brigade (Plate H2). This camel corps, plus a Sikh 'driver' for each camel, had been sent south to join the Central India Field Force, and rendered decisive service at the Battle of Kalpi. According to a J.N. Crealock sketch, these men had benefited from the mass production at Cawnpore in the winter of 1857–58 of sun helmets, which hitherto had been a rarity in Central India and non-existent among the troops from England.

Among the latter were two non-kilted Highland regiments, HM 71st and 72nd (see Plate H1). By 1859 some of the latter had also become camel-mounted, wearing the ship's smocks adopted during the 1858 hot weather, their tartan trews or brown trousers, and long turbans rolled round their caps with the ends hanging loose behind. The 71st abandoned their doublets and trews soon after arriving at Bombay in February and, according to their regimental history, marched to join the Central India Field Force in 'loose, pyjama-like suits dyed in curry powder', the resulting colour being described by Sylvester as 'lavender'. The regimental history says their head-dress was forage caps with peaks, covers and curtains, but Sylvester called it 'shako-shaped', suggesting the regiment's dress caps were under the covers. The only English regiment from home, for which there is ample evidence from J.N. Crealock's sketches and journal, was his own 95th (Plate H3).

A sizeable element of the forces engaged in Central India came from EIC Bombay Army, Euro-pean and Native, and to a lesser extent from Madras. The Bombay Artillery, Horse and Foot, provided much of the gunner support. A gunner of a horse troop is shown as Plate G3, based on J.N. Crealock, who also sketched a field battery dressed similarly but with covered forage caps. Sylvester recorded the 3rd Bombay Europeans as being dressed much like HM 71st, but specifically mentioned their forage caps with pagris round them, making a distinction with what he described as the 71st's headgear. A more marked contrast appeared in Crealock's drawings between, on the one hand, the ship's smocks of HM 72nd and 95th and, on the other, the regulation dress of white-covered forage caps and red coatees of the Bombay sepoy regiments and the 'cavalry grey' undress uniforms of the Bombay Light Cavalry.

Summary

The Indian Mutiny operations were the first in which British soldiers in large numbers fought and marched in clothing of lighter materials and of very different, more practical colouring than those traditionally worn on active service before 1857. Though influ-enced to some slight extent by the drab clothing worn hitherto on the North-West Frontier by such as the Punjab Irregular Force, its adoption was mainly due to the oppressive heat in which much of the fighting took place and in which, in peacetime, the British soldier had scarcely moved. Even so, some had to fight in their cloth uniforms, having been provided with no alternative. These uniforms were considered quite suitable for the so-called cold season, itself often hotter than an English summer.

Although the lightweight clothing became gener-ally known as 'khaki', its many shades and hues bore

Naval Brigade 24-pdr. gun in action during the advance to Fatehgarh, January 1858. (After Captain O. Jones, RN)

little resemblance to the colour known later by that name and worn by many armies, and derived solely from the rudimentary and different methods of dyeing white material, which otherwise became so quickly soiled. It was not adopted from any considerations of concealment for its wearer – then an unknown concept, despite the increased range and accuracy of rifled weapons – though its advantages in that regard over red or white were occasionally perceived as being instrumental in saving life and achieving surprise. That there was no express intent to give the soldier a specific 'service dress', as an alternative to his parade and working dress, can be seen by the fact that, after the Mutiny, all such dress disappeared from British regiments and was not seen again on active service for another 20 years.

CONCLUSION

The historian of the Royal and EIC Artilleries in the Mutiny categorised its military operations into battles, sieges, defences, captures, actions, skirmishes and 'affairs'. He listed by name a total of 180 between 11 May 1857 and 9 October 1859 in which gunners had taken part. Since gunners always acted in concert with cavalry or infantry, and usually both, this total can be taken as representing the fighting experienced by all arms; but this does not reflect the thousands of miles marched, in exhausting conditions, to engage the enemy.

Under the circumstances the battle casualties of EIC forces were not unduly high, though of course many more succumbed to heat or sickness. The siege of Delhi was by far the most costly, its totals of killed and wounded, 3,897, exceeding those incurred at Lucknow (its defence, two reliefs and capture – 2,962) and in Central India (654)[1] combined. Of these totals, 36% were sustained by loyal Native troops; at Delhi, where they provided just over half the force, the figure was 43%. The highest regimental casualties were the 389 killed and wounded suffered by HM 60th Rifles and 319 by the Sirmoor Goorkhas at Delhi, and the 377 lost by HM 32nd Foot while defending the Lucknow Residency: figures representing 50% or more of each battalion's strength, excluding casualties sustained elsewhere or from other causes.

Nowadays the Indian Mutiny tends to be regarded by the unthinking, as merely one of the very numerous 19th-century 'colonial' campaigns, of no more significance than, say, the Gordon Relief Expedition or the Pathan Revolt of 1897, and considerably less than the Zulu War. This is to forget what was at stake for Britain and her Army: no less than the saving of her position and prestige in

---

1 Excluding the 1857 operations and the Rajputana and Malwa Field Forces.

Types of the Delhi Field Force. From left: EIC Kumaon Gurkhas, HM 60th Rifles, EIC Bengal Horse Artillery, HM 75th Foot, HM 9th Lancers, EIC 2nd Bengal European Fusiliers. (After Captain G.F. Atkinson)

India – on which much of her reputation in the world depended – and, indeed, what was at stake for those who rebelled. It is also to undervalue the sheer scale of the two-year effort required to suppress it, whether in active operations or the maintenance of security in less affected areas: over half the entire British Army, together with thousands of loyal EIC soldiers, European and Native – the largest deployment of troops between the Napoleonic War and the South African War of 1899. When to all this is added the astonishing fortitude and bravery (epitomised by the awards of 182 Victoria Crosses) that was displayed, much of it in the hottest season of the year, by men not born to the climate and often unsuitably clad – then it must surely be acknowledged that, for the British soldier, the Indian Mutiny was rather more than just another 'colonial campaign'.

Its successful conclusion ended the East India Company's rule, but led to the foundation of our Indian Empire which would last for nearly another 100 years; and to a reformed, reorganised Indian Army, which was to give such distinguished service for the rest of the century and in two World Wars.

Yet for all that, the regiments that fought the Mutiny were only awarded the three Battle Honours of 'Delhi', 'Lucknow' or 'Central India'; and the men who did the work, one campaign medal with, at most, five bars.

Above: HM 61st Foot at Delhi; Surgeon Reade tending the wounded under fire just before he won the VC for leading an assault. (Watercolour by A.C. Lovett)

HM 52nd Light Infantry storming the Kashmir Gate, Delhi, 14 Sept. 1857.

THE PLATES

A: Mutineers:
1: Sowar, EIC 2nd Bengal Light Cavalry
2: Subadar, EIC 12th Bengal Native Infantry
3: Sepoy, EIC 54th Bengal Native Infantry

This plate complements those (E–G) in MAA 219. It depicts three examples of the Regular regiments of the Bengal Army, which provided the backbone of the insurgents. In the background is part of the Lucknow skyline.

All ten regiments of Bengal Light Cavalry were uniformed in 'French grey' with orange facings, except the 5th with black facings. *A1*, whose regiment mutinied at Cawnpore, is in mixed uniform and native dress, being based on a pencil drawing attributed to Captain Atkinson, Bengal Engineers, and his lithographs of the Delhi campaign.

A2, based on a British officer's drawing, shows a Native officer of the 12th BNI, which mutinied at Nowgong and Jhansi, in regulation dress as befitted one of those who, having given their loyalty to their sepoys rather than their British officers, found themselves commanding the companies and battalions which had mutinied.

A3, whose regiment mutinied at Delhi, is based on a description by Captain Richard Barter, HM 75th Foot, and wears his regulation hot-weather undress but with a dhoti instead of trousers, as most sepoys preferred. His firearm is the 1842 percussion musket.

B: Delhi:
1: Officer, EIC Bengal Artillery
2: Corporal, HM 1st Bn, 60th King's Royal Rifle Corps
3: Sepoy, EIC 4th Punjab Infantry

This and Plate C include representatives of Queen's and loyal EIC regiments in the Delhi Field Force. In the background is Flagstaff Tower, a prominent landmark on Delhi Ridge.

B1 is based on a photograph of Lieutenant E.T. Hume, who served at the siege with 1st Company, 4th Battalion, Bengal Artillery. His wadded coat was a popular garment among officers in India in the mid-19th century. His helmet is one of several types, more prevalent at this stage of the Mutiny among EIC officers than Queen's officers.

B2, whose battalion had been in India since 1845, is based on an Atkinson sketch. The crumpled nature of his cap cover suggests he has bound a turban round his forage cap inside it as added protection from sun and sword cuts. Despite the heat before Delhi, there is evidence that 1/60th adhered to its rifle-green, at least when on duty, hence his cold-weather shell jacket. 1/60th had the long pattern Enfield rifle at Delhi, not receiving the short version stipulated for rifle regiments (see H2) until the following year.

Captain Charles Gough, EIC Guides Cavalry, with his brother, Lieutenant Hugh Gough (right), and Captain Hodson (back view), both EIC Hodson's Horse, clearing a house at Khurkowdah, 15 Aug. 1857. Both Goughs won the VC, Charles for this occasion and four others, Hugh at Lucknow. Painting by W. Desanges. (National Army Museum)

B3, a Pathan from one of the Punjab Irregular Force battalions, is based on a lithograph after Captain Fane and a drawing by W. Carpenter. This battalion later served in the Lucknow operations. He wears the all-khaki clothing and brown leather equipment of most PIF regiments. His rifle is the Brunswick with sword bayonet, for which a hammer, attached by a cord to the pouch belt, was issued to assist the loading process.

C: Delhi:
1: Private, EIC 2nd (Bengal European) Fusiliers
2: Sepoy, EIC Sirmoor Battalion
3: Officer, HM 75th Regiment

Both regiments of Bengal Fusiliers (Europeans) were at Delhi, the 2nd having their white shirts and trousers dyed a brownish khaki as in *C1*, the 1st's clothing being of a greyish hue (see MAA 198, Plate A2). The fusiliers appear to have retained their shoulder belt plates, which had been abolished in Queen's regiments. His firearm is the 1842 percussion musket with socket bayonet, its caps being carried in the small brown pouch on the waistbelt.

Of the two Gurkha local battalions at Delhi, Captain Medley, Bengal Engineers, recorded that the Sirmoor Battalion (later 2nd Goorkha Rifles) kept to its rifle-green uniform, as in *C2*. Like Queen's Rifle regiments (B2, H2), its accoutrements were of black leather. It is difficult to tell from the drawing on which this figure is based with what firearm the battalion was armed, other than its having a socket bayonet; but a photograph of the Nussuree Battalion at the time shows a weapon that resembles the rifled musket with 2-ft. 9-in. barrel ordered in 1840 for Foot Guards' sergeants (see MAA 193, p.24).

C3 is based on descriptions by Captain Barter, 75th. This regiment, stationed in India since 1849, had left its peacetime quarters for Delhi with only its white drill undress jackets and trousers, which were dyed en route, the result being 'slate-coloured'. Barter mentions the 75th officers' shell jackets having turned-down collars. For the assault on Delhi, Barter tied two turbans round his covered forage cap 'for protection going up the ladders', and all the 75th officers discarded their sword scabbards, hence this figure's sword slings being buckled together. His sword is the 1822 infantry pattern and his revolver the 1855 Adams. After the fall of Delhi the 75th, together with HM 8th, who were similarly dressed, subsequently took part in the second relief of Lucknow, both regiments still in their slate-coloured clothing, by then in a tattered condition.

In the background is Delhi's Lahore Gate.

D: Oudh: First Relief of Lucknow (Sept. 1857):
1: Private, HM 32nd (Cornwall) Regiment
2: Sergeant, HM 90th (Perthshire Volunteers) Light Infantry
3: Officer, EIC Madras European Fusiliers

$D1$'s regiment, in India since 1846, was the mainstay of the defence of the Lucknow Residency from June 1857 until reinforced by Havelock's column in September. This was the hottest time of the year, hence $D1$ is in his forage cap with a turban around it, as Private Metcalfe of the regiment recorded, his once-white shell jacket and dungaree working trousers. References by Metcalfe to 'muskets' suggest that the 32nd had not yet received the Enfield rifle, so $D1$ has the 1842 pattern.

$D2$, based on a watercolour by Lieutenant Sankey, Madras Engineers, and $D3$, from photographs, were both in Havelock's column. $D2$'s regiment had left England as part of the China expedition, having been issued with forage cap covers and the brown 'boat-coats' before departure. With this $D2$ wears regulation home service summer trousers. He is armed with the short Enfield with sword bayonet ordered for his rank, and has a whistle attached by chains to his pouch belt as worn by light infantry sergeants. Part of the 90th were shipwrecked during the voyage out and lost all their kit, reaching India later (see main text).

For the advance from Calcutta up to Oudh, the formidable Colonel Neill equipped his Madras Fusiliers ($D3$) with white frocks and blue forage cap covers, thereby earning the Regiment's nickname of 'Neill's Blue Caps'. At some stage the frocks must have been dyed, as they appear in markedly contrasting shades in some photographs. During the cold season of 1857–58 the regiment received 'red quilted tunics', according to the Regimental History. $D3$ wears his sword belt under his frock, a common practice when not in full dress. All his fusiliers were armed with Enfields.

In the background is the Lucknow Residency.

E: Oudh: Second Relief of Lucknow (Nov.), Cawnpore (Dec.), Final Capture of Lucknow (March 1858):
1: Private, HM 53rd (Shropshire) Regiment
2: Private, HM 9th (Queen's Royal) Lancers
3: Officer, Royal Navy

Sir Colin Campbell's force, which relieved and then evacuated the enlarged garrison of Lucknow, included, *inter alia*, HM 53rd ($E1$), in India since 1844, some regiments from Delhi like $E2$, $B3$ and $C3$, and a

HM 5th Fusiliers at the Alambagh, Lucknow, 24 Sept. 1857; Corporal Grant winning the VC for rescuing Private Deveney, whose leg had been shot off during a reconnaissance. (Modern painting by David Rowlands for the Royal Regiment of Fusiliers)

Naval Brigade under Captain Peel VC, RN. A portrait of the latter at the third battle of Cawnpore includes the figure of Private Hannaford of the 53rd which, together with a drawing by Captain O. Jones RN, forms the basis of *E1* – in covered forage cap, red tunic and white trousers. The 53rd, one of only three Foot regiments with red facings, was at all three actions covered in this plate.

HM 9th Lancers (*E2*) had fought through the siege of Delhi in their white undress which, unlike other Delhi regiments, was not dyed. From 4 October they changed to their home service tunics, as here, officers wearing their cloth stable jackets. The forage cap covers had been dyed in September and to these were added white turbans. The 9th, which won 12 VCs during the Mutiny, was always noted by eyewitnesses for the 'perfection' of their 'well-dressed and clean appearance', achieved by a 'proper strictness about uniform', which marked them as 'a gallant, dashing, always-to-the-front' regiment. E2 is armed with the 1853 universal pattern sword and 9-ft. ash lance without lange-flag, which has been discarded after Delhi. The 9th wore this dress in both the November and March Lucknow operations.

E3 is based on a self-portrait by Captain O. Jones RN, who served as a volunteer in Campbell's force, mainly with the 53rd and Naval Brigade, at Lucknow's final capture. Being usually mounted he wears riding boots, but illustrations of Peel and his other officers show them in loose white trousers. Most wore covered forage caps but Peel favoured an airpipe helmet. Ratings wore their Sennet straw hats with white covers, blue blouses and white trousers.

F: Oudh and Rohilkand (March–Aug. 1858):
1: Driver, Royal Horse Artillery
2: Corporal, HM 79th (Cameron) Highlanders
3: Rissaldar, EIC Hodson's Horse

Among the reinforcements from England that formed much of Campbell's army were horse troops and field batteries of the Royal Regiment of Artillery,

HM 93rd Highlanders storming the Sikandarbagh, Lucknow, 16 Nov. 1857: watercolour by Orlando Norie. (National Army Museum)

Officers and men of EIC 1st European Bengal Fusiliers with T.H. Kavanagh VC (in helmet) *after the capture of Lucknow. (Private collection)*

Below: HM 9th Lancers attacking mutineers: watercolour by Orlando Norie. (Anne S.K. Brown Military Collection)

*Sir Colin Campbell and
staff watching HM 5th
Fusiliers (all ranks now in
helmets) skirmishing at*
*Dundeakhera, 24 Nov.
1858: drawing by Colonel
H.H. Crealock. (National
Army Museum)*

which had not served in India for many years. *F1*,
from a photograph, is in RHA home service dress
with a turban rolled round his forage cap, his whip
and right leg guard denoting his rank of driver.

HM 79th Highlanders (*F2*) reached India in late
1857. The Regimental Records state that, after
fighting at Lucknow in red, they changed to ship's
smocks dyed light blue, as here, before the Rohilkand
campaign. Quilted sunshades for the feather bonnets
were issued, as well as light blue muslin pagris for
their Glengarries. Despite their size the bonnets were
a practical headdress for India, affording some shade
from the tails and, if the inner skull was removed (as
practised by the 93rd Highlanders), permitting air to
blow through the feathers. The leather-covered soda-
water bottles were issued on the regiment's arrival at
Calcutta. The rifle is the Enfield. The tartan was
Cameron of Erracht, and the red and green hose were
peculiar to the 79th.

Hodson's Horse was an Irregular cavalry regiment raised in the Punjab, largely from Sikhs, in May
1857 by Lieutenant W.S.R. Hodson, formerly of the
Bengal Fusiliers and the Guides. It was present at
Delhi, the second relief and capture of Lucknow, and
subsequent operations in Oudh. Although the uniform was generally khaki, photographs, on which *F3*
is based, show considerable variety of clothing and
weapons, the regiment being chiefly distinguished by
its red pagris and cummerbunds. The Regimental
History states that red shoulder sashes were also

worn; these are visible in one Atkinson lithograph,
but not in another, nor are they evident in the
photographs. *F3* is armed with a native 'tulwar' and
'pepperbox' pistol.

G: Central India (Jan.–June 1858):
1: Private, HM 14th (The King's) Light Dragoons
2: Officer, HM 86th (Royal County Down) Regiment
3: Gunner, EIC Bombay Horse Artillery

The 14th Light Dragoons had been in India since
1841 and had recently returned from the Persian War
of 1856–57. According to regimental accounts they
had for years worn turbans with one end hanging
down to protect the neck, except on full dress
occasions, hence their nickname of 'Pagri-Wallahs'.
With these, in Central India, they initially wore their
cloth tunics open at the neck, but with the onset of the
hot weather they marched in shirt-sleeves, as here, or
blouses dyed with curry powder. *G1* is armed with
the 1821 light cavalry sword and Victoria pattern
carbine. The 14th were constantly on operations in
Central India from June 1857 until late summer
1858. Note the salute of the period.

The 86th (*G2*) played a major part in the

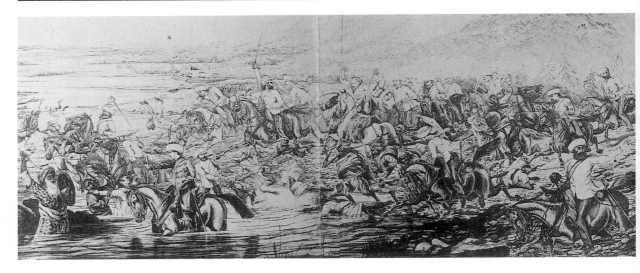

HM 7th Hussars charging rebels on the Raptee river, Oudh-Nepal border, 31 Dec. 1858: drawing by Colonel H.H. Crealock. (National Army Museum)

storming of Jhansi (in background) on 3 April 1858 and at Gwalior, 19–20 June. This officer is in his regulation undress shell jacket and cotton trousers dyed dark blue, according to the recollections of a regimental officer, J.G. Dartnell. His helmet, made in Bombay, was of leather with a white cotton cover and pagri. In the earlier, November 1857, Central India operations the men of the 86th were seen wearing their tunics and shakos with white covers, but later adopted forage caps with covers and curtains, worn with red shell jackets by night or when cold, and grey woollen shirts with sleeves rolled up in the heat of the day.

G3 is based on a drawing by Lieutenant J.N. Crealock, HM 95th, and wears the Roman-type helmet used with different embellishments by all three EIC Horse Artillery regiments, within a white cover, together with his cold-weather stable jacket and leather-reinforced trousers. Three troops of this regiment went through the Central India campaign.

H: Central India (March–Sept. 1858):
1: Private, HM 72nd (Duke of Albany's Own) Highlanders
2: Private, HM Rifle Brigade (Camel Corps)
3: Private, HM 95th (Derbyshire) Regiment

H1's regiment reached India in January 1858. Regimental records state that they marched initially in feather bonnets, red doublets and dungaree trousers; but when encamped before Kotah in March a sketch by Lieutenant E.J. Upton shows the trousers to have been replaced by all ranks with their regimental tartan (Prince Charles Edward Stuart) trews. For the assault on Kotah on the 29th the feather bonnets gave way to covered forage caps, as here. The latter were retained thereafter when the doublets were exchanged for ship's smocks (as in F2), dyed an 'earthy-brown' (see MAA 198, p.33).

H2 is one of 200 riflemen who, with two companies of HM 88th, formed the Camel Corps organised in April 1858. He is in the cotton clothing, with regimental facings, adopted after their rifle-green was discarded following Lucknow's capture, and one of the sun helmets mass-produced at Cawnpore. He is based on a J.N. Crealock sketch showing one such rifleman mounted on his camel behind its Sikh driver, who has a black band round his turban, and another soldier with white equipment who must be 88th, whose Sikh has a pale band, probably yellow to match the 88th's facings.

The appearance of Crealock's own regiment (*H3*), which reached India in early 1858, features in his sketches and journal. At Kotah they were in covered forage caps, red shell jackets and dungaree trousers, which were worn up to May, but by June white ship's smocks had replaced the shells. Crealock described them marching on Gwalior: '500 bearded, sunburnt men, in once-white sea kit smocks, tattered blue trousers, here and there bare feet, here and there native slippers, while for headdress the Kilmarnock forage cap with white cover did duty, sometimes assisted by a towel or roll of coloured cotton'—a description he supplemented with a sketch, which forms the basis of H3. When the men adopted smocks the officers retained their red shells for a while, but then changed to loose grey-blue frocks. At Gwalior one officer wore a black velvet hunting cap with a blue towel rolled round it.

The rifles of all three figures are Enfields, the rifleman having the short version also carried by all sergeants. In the background is the fortress of Gwalior, the capture of which largely ended the Central India campaign except for mopping-up operations.

HM 72nd Highlanders entering Kotah, Rajputana, 30 March 1858: sketch by Lieutenant E.J. Upton, 72nd. (Queen's Own Highlanders)

Bibliography

Annand, A. McK (ed.), *Cavalry Surgeon: Recollections of J.H. Sylvester* (1971)

Anson, Maj. O.H.S.G., *With HM 9th Lancers During the Indian Mutiny* (1896)

Atkinson, Capt. G.F., *The Campaign in India 1857–58* (1859)

Barter, Lt.-Gen. Richard, *Mutiny Memories: The Siege of Delhi* (1984)

Blomfield, David (ed.), *Lahore to Lucknow: Indian Mutiny Journal of A.M. Lang* (1992)

Butler, Sir Lewis, *Annals of the KRRC, Vol. III* (1926)

Cardew, Maj. F. G., *Hodson's Horse* (1928)

Cope, Sir William, *History of the Rifle Brigade* (1877)

Dawson, Capt. L., *Squires and Sepoys* (1960)

Duberly, Mrs Henry, *Campaigning in Rajpootana and Central India* (1859)

Edwardes, Michael, *Battle of the Indian Mutiny* (1963)

Edwardes, Michael, *A Season in Hell: Defence of Lucknow* (1973)

Forbes-Mitchell, W., *Reminiscences of the Great Mutiny* (1894)

Griffiths, C.J., *Narrative of the Siege of Delhi* (1910)

Hibbert, C., *The Great Mutiny* (1978)

Jocelyn, Col. J.R.J., *History of the Royal and Indian Artillery in the Mutiny* (1915)

Jones, Capt. O., *Recollections of a Winter Campaign in India, 1857–58* (1859)

Kaye, Sir J.W., *History of the Sepoy War, 1857–58 (3 vols)* (1880)

Laurie, Lt.-Col. G.B., *History of the Royal Irish Rifles* (1914)

Leask, J.C., *Historical Records of the QO Cameron Highlanders* (1909)

MacMunn, Lt.-Gen. Sir G., *The Indian Mutiny in Perspective* (1931)

Medley, J.G., *A Year's Campaign in India* (1858)

Mollo, B., *The Indian Army* (1981)

Muter, Mrs, *My Recollections of the Sepoy Revolt* (1911)

Perkins, R., *The Kashmir Gate* (1983)

Raines, Gen. Sir J., *The 95th in Central India* (1900)

Russell, W.H., *My Diary in India (2 vols)* (1860)

Tuker, Lt.-Gen. Sir F., *Chronicle of Private Henry Metcalfe, HM 32nd Foot* (1953)

Wylly, H.C., *Neill's Blue Caps* (1925)

Journal of the Society for Army Historical Research (1921–93)

Notes sur les planches en couleurs

A Régiments réguliers de l'armée de Bengale, d'où venaient la majorité des mutiniers. A1 Adapté d'une gravure de Atkinson: les dix régiments de cavalerie portaient tous cet uniforme 'gris français', neuf d'entre eux avec des parements orange. Ce soldat de cavalerie a remplacé certains éléments de son uniforme par des vêtements régionaux. A2 Uniforme réglementaire conservé par les officiers autochtones qui participèrent à la mutinerie. A3 D'après des témoignages: petite tenue réglementaire par temps chaud, mais avec un *dhoti* à la place du pantalon. L'arme standard était le mousquet à canon lisse à amorces de 1842.

B Troupes de la Reine et troupes loyales à la East India Company durant le siège de Delhi, à partir de photographies et d'esquisses. B1 La veste molletonnée et le casque sont plus représentatifs des officiers de la Company que de ceux de la Reine à cette époque. Le casque pare-soleil commençait à peine à faire son apparition dans différentes versions achetées par les individus eux-mêmes. B2 Il semble que le calot ait été agrémenté d'un turban pour la protection contre le soleil et contre les coups. Les *Rifles* (fusiliers) conservaient leur veste blindée vert foncé même dans la chaleur de l'été, ils étaient en Inde depuis plus de dix ans. L'arme est le fusil Linfield de taille infanterie. B3 Uniforme de terrain pratique d'aspect 'moderne', pour l'été, porté par un Pathan des troupes loyales du *Punjab Irregular Force*.

C Unités supplémentaires qui participèrent aux combats à Delhi. C1 Unité européenne d'infanterie de la Company recrutée sur place. Ce bataillon teignit des chemises et pantalons blancs en marron clair et le 1er Bat. en gris clair. C2 Les Gurkhas loyaux de cette unité (devinrent tard les 2e fusiliers Gurkhas) conservèrent leur uniforme vert de temps froid avec du matériel en cuir noir. Nous ne sommes pas certains de l'arme, peut-être un mousquet rayé à barillet court comme celui qui fut émis en 1840 aux individus des Foot Guards. C3 Cette unité, qui était en Inde depuis longtemps, teignit sa petite tenue 'couleur ardoise'. Les officiers abaissaient leur col et durant l'assaut se débarrassaient du fourreau de l'épée de 1822. Son révolver est un Adams.

D Relève de Lucknow. D1 Cette unité formait la garnison principale de juin à septembre 1857. Les turbans étaient souvent utilisés pour leur confort et pour protéger quelque peu la tête. Il porte une veste d'été de petite tenue qui fut blanche et un pantalon *dungaree*. D2 D'après une aquarelle de la colonne de secours de Havelock. Notez le 'boat coat' distribué pour l'expédition chinoise sur laquelle on préleva plusieurs unités pour les envoyer en Inde et le pantalon d'été du service domestique, le fusil court Enfield et la baïonnette-épée d'un sergent ainsi que le sifflet d'un sergent d'infanterie légère. D3 Unité européenne locale qui portait des 'tenues' teintées sur place dans différentes couleurs et le protège-calot bleu.

E Opérations plus tardives autour de Lucknow et de Cawnpore, hiver 1857–58. E1 D'après trois toiles d'époque; les 53ème étaient en Inde depuis 1844. Ils étaient une des rares unités d'infanterie portant des parements rouges à leur tunique. E2 Cette unité connue pour son élégance, les 9èmes Lanciers, portaient un blanc non teinté en été et des tuniques de service domestique en hiver agrémentées d'un turban. E3 D'après un auto-portrait, les officiers de marine portaient des bottes de cheval durant les marches, mais d'autres sources montrent un pantalon blanc large. La majorité portait un calot et quelques-uns une version préliminaire du casque pare-soleil.

F1 La majorité des soldats de l'armée de Colin Campbell étaient des renforts d'Angleterre; notez l'uniforme de service domestique agrémenté d'un turban. F2 Après avoir combattu à Lucknow en tunique rouge, ce régiment adopta des 'smocks de marine' teints en bleu ciel, comme ici. Un pare-soleil molletonné fut ajouté au bonnet des Highlands qui était assez léger et frais une fois que l'on enlevait la partie interne. Des bouteilles d'eau de seltz recouvertes de cuir étaient souvent utilisées comme cantines en Inde. F3 Célèbre unité de cavalerie irrégulière qui portait différents vêtements, généralement kaki, mais qui se distinguait par ses turbans et ses ceintures rouges.

G1 Les 14èmes Dragons légers, qui restèrent en Inde pendant plus de vingt ans, portaient le turban depuis longtemps. Par temps chaud ils montaient à cheval en chemise. Leurs armes étaient l'épée de cavalerie légère de 1821 et la carabine Victoria. G2 Des mémoires décrivent les officiers du 86ème en veste blindée réglementaire et pantalon de coton teints en bleu foncé, avec un casque de cuir couvert en blanc et un turban. G3 Des gravures et les règlements indiquent l'usage du casque romain dans les unités d'artillerie montée de la Company, porté ici avec une veste d'écurie pour temps froid et un pantalon renforcé de cuir.

H1 A leur arrivée en 1858, les 73èmes se battirent d'abord en poupoint rouge, en pantalon (trews) écossais et en bonnet à plumes, ce dernier remplacé par un calot pour les assauts. H2 Un des 200 fusiliers rattachés à un corps à dos de chameau en avril 1858. Il porte des vêtements en coton avec parements régimentaires, qui remplacèrent l'uniforme vert foncé après Lucknow et un casque pare-soleil d'un type fabriqué en quantité à Cawnpore. H3 Comme la figure précédente, provient d'une esquisse de Crealock d'un uniforme de campagne d'été: 'smock de marine' qui fut blanc, *dungarees* bleu mal en point, calot avec couvre-calot et/ou turban et fusil Enfield et matériel.

Farbtafeln

A Stehende Regimenter der Bengalischen Armee, aus der der Großteil der Meuterer stammte. A1 Nach einer Zeichnung von Atkinson: alle zehn Kavallerie-Regimenter trugen diese 'französisch-graue' Uniform, neun davon hatten orangefarbene Einfassung. A2 Deinstuniform, die einheimische Offiziere, die sich den Meuterern anschlossen, beibehielten. A3 Nach Augenzeugenberichten: die vorschriftsmäßige 'Interimsuniform' für warmes Wetter, hier mit einem *Dhoti* anstelle der Hosen. Die Standardwaffe war die 1842er Perkussionsflinte mit glattem Lauf.

B Truppen der Queen's und der loyalen Ostindien-Kompanie bei der Belagerung von Delhi, nach Fotos und Zeichnungen. B1 Die wattierte Jacke und der Helm sind zu dieser Zeit eher für die Kompanie- als für Queen's-Offiziere typisch. Der Tropenhelm hielt gerade Einzug, und zwar in individuell angeschafften Versionen. B2 Unter dem Bezug scheint ein Turban um das Käppi gewunden zu sein, was zum Schutz vor der Sonne und Hieben diente. Die *Rifles* behielten die dunkelgrüne, leichte Offiziersjacke auch in der Sommerhitze an; sie waren bereits seit über zehn Jahren in Indien. Bei der Waffe handelt es sich um das Enfield-Gewehr in voller Infanterie-Länge. B3 'Modern' erscheinende, praktische Feldbekleidung für den Sommer, hier an einem pathan der loyalen *Punjab Irregular Force*.

C Andere Einheiten, die in Delhi kämpften. C1 Vor Ort rekrutierte, europäische Einheit der Kompanie-Infanterie. Dieses Bataillon färbte weiße Hemden und Hosen hellbraun, das 1. Bn. hellgrau. C2 Die loyalen Gurkhas dieser Einheit (später die *2nd Gurkha Rifles*) behielten ihre grüne Uniform für kaltes Wetter und die schwarze Lederausrüstung. Die Waffe ist unsicher – unter Umständen die Gewehrmuskete mit kurzem Lauf, wie sie 1840 an die Sergeanten des Garderegiments ausgegeben wurde. C3 Diese Einheit ist seit langem in Indien und man weiß, daß sie weiße Interimsuniformen 'schieferfarben' einfärbte. Die Offiziere schlugen den Kragen um und entledigten sich zum Gefecht der Scheide des 1822er Schwerts; sein Revolver ist ein Adams.

D Ablösung in Lucknow. D1 Diese Einheit stellte von Juni bis September 1857 die Hauptbesatzung dar. Es wurde oft ein Turban getragen, da er bequem war und einen gewissen Schutz bot. Er trägt eine ehemals weiße Interimssommerjacke und *Dungaree*-Hosen. D2 Von einem Aquarell der Hilfskolonne von Havelock. Man beachte die 'Bootsjacke', die für die China-Expedition ausgegeben wurde, von der mehrere Einheiten nach Indien überstellt wurden, und die Sommerhosen der Bürgerwehr; die kurze Enfield-Gewehr und das Säbelbajonett eines Sergeanten und die Trillerpfeife eines Sergeanten der leichten Infanterie. D3 Örtliche, europäische Einheit, die vor Ort gefärbte 'Kittel' in verschiedenen Farbtönen trug, und ein blaues Käppi.

E Spätere Einsätze um Lucknow und Cawnpore im Winter 1857–58. E1 Zwei Gemälden der Zeit nachempfunden; der 53rd war seit 1844 in Indien stationiert. Sie war eine der wenigen Infanterie-Einheiten, die an der Jacke rote Regiments-Einfassungen trug. E2 Die *9th Lancers* waren eine bemerkenswert gut gekleidete Einheit und trugen im Sommer ungefärbtes Weiß und im Winter Jacken der Bürgerwehr mit gefärbtem Käppi und zusätzlichem Turban. E3 Nach einem Selbstporträt; Marineoffiziere trugen auf dem Marsch Reitstiefel, doch sieht man auf anderen Abbildungen lose, weiße Hosen. Die meisten trugen bezogene Käppis, einige eine frühe Version des Tropenhelms.

F1 Beim Großteil der Armee von Colin Campbell handelte es sich um Verstärkungen aus England; man beachte die Uniform der Bürgerwehr mit zusätzlichem Turban. F2 Nach dem Gefecht in Lucknow wechselte dieses Regiment von der roten Uniformjacke zu 'Matrosenkitteln' über, die wie hier hellblau gefärbt waren; der Highland-Kappe wurde ein gesteppter Sonnenschutz hinzugefügt. Die Kopfbedeckung war recht leicht und kühl, wenn man das Innenfutter herausnahm. In Indien wurden für gewöhnlich lederbezogene Sodawasserflaschen als Feldflaschen benutzt. F3 Berühmte, irreguläre Kavallerie-Einheit, die verschiedene, meist khakifarbene Kleidung trug, doch durch rote Turbane und Schärpen erkenntlich war.

G1 Die *14th Light Dragoons* waren seit fast 20 Jahren in Indien und trugen seit langem einen Turban; bei warmem Wetter ritten sie nur im Hemd. Bei den Waffen handelt es sich um den 1821er leichten Kavallerie-Säbel und die Victoria-Karabiner. G2 In Memoiren werden Offiziere des 86th in vorschriftsmäßigen leichten Uniformjacken und Baumwollhosen, die dunkelblau gefärbt waren, beschrieben und in Lederhelmen mit weißem Bezug und Turban. G3 Zeichnungen und Akten verweisen auf den romanischen Helm der Pferde-Artillerie-Einheiten der Kompanie, der hier mit Kaltwetterjacken und lederverstärkten Hosen getragen wird.

H1 Das 72nd stieß 1858 dazu und kämpfte zunächst in rotem Wams, karierten Schottenhosen und befiederten Mützen, die beim Gefecht durch dieses Käppi ersetzt wurden. H2 Einer der 200 Schützen die im April 1858 einem Kameltrupp zugeteilt wurden; er trägt Baumwollkleidung mit Regimentseinfassung, die nach Lucknow an die Stelle der dunkelgrünen Uniform trat, und einen Tropenhelm eines Modells, das in Cawnpore in großen Mengen hergestellt wurde. H3 Nach einem vorhergehenden Abbildung stammt auch diese von einer Crealock-Zeichnung des Sommerfeldanzugs: ehemals weißer 'Matrosenkittel', zerschlissens, blaue *Dungarees*, Käppi mit Bezug und/oder Turban und Enfield-Gewehr und Koppel.